C000015711

TALKING
THE TALK

Top Tips on
how to be a Confident
and Dynamic Speaker

First published in 2013 by Speaking Words
Piglet Barn, Manor Road, North Walsham, Norfolk NR28 9LH
www.speakingwords.co.uk

Typesetting and layout by Rocket Design (East Anglia), Park House,
21 Yarmouth Road, North Walsham, Norfolk NR28 9AT

Proofreading and copy-editing by Sarah Cheeseman

©Andrew Brammer. All rights reserved.

Andrew Brammer has asserted his rights under the Copyright, Designs and
Patents Act 1988 to be identified as the author of this work.

No part of this book may be reproduced in any form or by any electronic or
mechanical means, including information storage or retrieval systems, without
the prior written permission of the publisher.

A CIP catalogue record for this book is available from the British Library.

ISBN: 978-0-9569627-2-0

Contents

About This Book

Being able to speak and present to groups and have real impact is such an important skill to have.

The best leaders, the best managers, the best motivators, the best at promoting their businesses, are those who can speak and present effectively in public. Not forgetting those who speak at conferences and events, and who have that amazing ability to wow and dazzle an audience.

And the skills and techniques you use in public speaking are totally transferable, and can be used in so many situations – yes, conferences and events, but also team briefings, staff reviews, sales presentations, networking events, impromptu situations, staff Q&A sessions, board meetings, radio and TV interviews. So, for those who may think, 'Oh, I don't need public speaking skills, I'll never have to give a speech,' think again!

You can, though, only learn public speaking and presenting by doing, not just from books or by someone standing there telling you how to do it. It's a bit like learning to drive a car. You get in the car, have lessons with an instructor, make mistakes, learn from these and improve, keep following this process until you become proficient, pass your test, and then learn to drive on your own until it becomes second nature.

Now, there are literally hundreds of books that have been written about public speaking and delivering presentations. And having said what I have about not being able to learn the craft just from books, I didn't think it would bring anything to the party by just rehashing another weighty tome on the subject.

So with this little book, I thought it would be a nice idea to put together a series of tips, techniques and ideas about what works and what perhaps doesn't when you are preparing for and then delivering a speech or presentation. It's an easy-to-read guide of some basic principles and practices to help you with your speaking proficiency – a bit like a Highway Code for public speaking and presentation skills. It will take you through a logical sequence of what to do from the moment you are asked to prepare a speech or presentation, right up to when you deliver it.

These, then, are some of the key practices I have picked up, followed and used during my many years of delivering and listening to speeches. They will be able to act as a quick reference guide for you, providing some handy tips at a glance, and a checklist to dip into and use as a refresher before you have to give a presentation, whether you're a complete novice or a more experienced presenter just needing a recap. And if you are a more experienced speaker, although some of this book may cover familiar ground, perhaps you can take away a couple of fresh nuggets and pearls of public speaking wisdom.

What I haven't included, though, is a specific section on, or much mention of, nerves (whoops! I've said it!), as I feel far too many books and courses draw attention to this area. Remember what I said about you only being able to learn public speaking by doing? Well, keep doing, follow the tips in this book that are appropriate to you, and you will minimise any nerves.

Having effective presentation skills is absolutely crucial in today's world, and if you are proficient in public speaking, you have a far greater chance of being successful in life.

And if you would like me to help you on your communication skills journey, whether you are at the very beginning or are further along the way, please feel free to get in touch with me, so that I can help you say, 'Wow! I can do that!'

Anyway, enough of the weighty introduction, let's get on with the short, sharp tips and techniques.

Being An Effective Public Speaker And Presenter Will Enable You To:

- Be more persuasive, influential and motivational
- Be more confident and self-assured, with an increased presence
- Manage and lead more effectively
- Be viewed in a positive and influential light by others
- Inspire greater creativity in yourself and others
- Articulate and get across your ideas more effectively
- Present your thoughts and ideas in a logical manner
- Win people over to your point of view
- Deliver better team briefings and workforce addresses
- Think and speak on your feet in impromptu situations
- Handle Q&A sessions
- Better manage difficult communication situations
- Chair events
- Deliver powerful and memorable speeches
- Be memorable – for all the right reasons
- Win more sales

Dedication
To The Craft

Some Good Things To Consider And To Remember

- Do you want to be like everyone else up on the speaking platform? Do you want to be bland and anonymous? Or, do you want to be different and remembered for all the right reasons?

- It can be said that there are essentially four types of speakers and presenters – those who don't want to get up there at all; those who do want to get up there, yet get off the platform as quickly as possible; those who want to get up there and do a technically efficient yet straightforward job; and those who want to get up there, be a bit different, make a real impression for themselves and / or their business and be memorable for all the right reasons. Which type do you want to be?

- Being memorable is one of the main qualities of being a powerful presenter.

- The first rule of public speaking is – there are no rules, only guidelines for best practice.

- If there were rules, and everyone spoke and delivered in the same way, we may as well just wheel robots onto the speaking platform.

- Don't be afraid to be different. Don't be afraid to take risks.

- Find what techniques work best for you, and then weave them into your own unique speaking and presenting style.

- When you're delivering a presentation, think of what Miles Davis said to his band: 'Play what you feel.'

- A speech is like an iceberg – what the audience see and hear is just the 10% above the surface. The hidden 90% below the surface is all the work and preparation you have put in beforehand.

- Would an Olympic athlete enter a race without training? Would a heart surgeon enter an operating theatre, or a pilot take the controls of a passenger jet, without being primed and ready for the task ahead? Should a speaker take to the platform without having prepared?

- As with sport, you will always get the outsider who rises to the occasion and wins a one-off event. But to be a consistent performer day in day out, week in week out, month in month out, year in year out, takes something else. With your speaking you want to aim to be that consistent performer.

- Always try to know inside out what you will be talking about – try to become an expert.

- Always prepare as much as you possibly can – but don't worry when the real world cuts in and has its say. For, in the real world, you don't always have the utopia of perfect or completely uninterrupted preparation.

- Gain and learn from experience, and take every available speaking opportunity you can, including impromptu situations. The more you speak in public, the more you will be able to prepare and structure presentations at very short notice, and also speak off the cuff. You will only learn from experience.

- If a radio station rang you up, say, at 9.00a.m. asking you to appear on air, would you be able to prepare and deliver a talk or a story by 3.00p.m. that same day? Or, if you arrived at an event expecting to speak for 10 minutes, and the organisers suddenly explain that they would like 45 minutes, would you be able to deliver? That's the level of proficiency and expertise you want to aim for.

- Take 3 minutes to write down everything that would contribute to an appalling presentation. Then write down and do everything opposite to this.

- Keep a journal – make notes, scribble ideas, jot down quotes. Always keep your creative mind alert.

- Don't be afraid to bounce speech ideas off people.

- At the end of the day, ask yourself, 'What have I done today to make myself a better speaker and presenter?'

Learning From Other Speakers

- Get into the habit of becoming a better listener. Learn how to constructively evaluate other people's speeches and presentations.

- Listen to and read great presentations and speeches. Listen to inspiring and brilliant speakers in all walks of life – business, political, social, humorous.

- Look, listen and learn from other speakers, and absorb like a sponge the best practices that appeal to you.

- Similarly, listen to terrible presentations and learn to avoid their worst aspects like the plague.

- Learn to understand why some presentations succeed and why some fail.

Benefiting From Feedback

■ Sift and evaluate feedback. Be honest with yourself, then pick out the bits you think are fair and that you think you can use to help you improve.

■ Learn from criticism and feedback, but don't take negative comments to heart.

■ Don't take things personally, or get deflated by unkind or critical comments.

■ Be aware of taking too much advice from others – don't change what your gut instinct says you should stick with.

■ Remember, you're never going to satisfy everyone all the time.

Your Speech
Or Presentation

What To Say

Selecting Your Subject

- Sometimes your subject will be set for you; sometimes it will be of your own choosing. The first things to ask yourself, though, are: what do you want to accomplish; what main message or points do you want to communicate?

- What, then, are the aims and objectives of your speech? Why will the audience be listening to you? For instance, is the audience looking to be entertained, educated, informed, inspired, motivated, moved, persuaded, trained, or a combination of these?

- Your aim is to achieve empathy with your audience. Put yourself in your listeners' shoes, pretend you are an audience member, and ask yourself, 'WIIFME – what's in it for me? What would I get from listening to this speech?'

- Think about the people who will be in the audience. What type of people will they be in terms of their age range, gender, occupation, income, education, lifestyle, political views, leisure interests, etc.?

- Will they prefer or be suited to a longer or shorter presentation? Do they have a sense of humour? If the audience is an organisation or a society, what sort of speakers have spoken to them before?

- You need to know from the outset how long you will be speaking for. This is crucial so that you can prepare and tailor your content accordingly.

- Before writing the detail of your speech, be able to summarise what it is about in a few sentences.

Writing Your Speech

- Research your subject – know what you are talking about!

- Be aware when writing your speech or presentation that the spoken word is quite different from the written word.

- Prepare and write your content to match how long you have been given for your speech.

- Remember – an audience does not want to be short-changed. Nor do they wish to be bored witless by a droning and overlong speech. Overrunning may also eat into other people's speaking time.

- Write a presentation with a length that is a fair bit under your allotted speaking slot time. This then removes any time pressure on you, and gives you the luxury of being able to perform without this pressure. So, for example, if your speaking slot is 15 minutes, write a 12-minute presentation – and then deliver it in 15 minutes.

- Write content that will engage and appeal to your audience, but which will be applicable to the occasion. Although a presentation should be as polished as possible, make sure your content and wording is natural and in your own style, so that it does not sound alien to you.

- Adapt your words to suit your audience. For instance, it wouldn't be advisable to use management gobbledygook in front of a shop floor gathering, or 'industrial style language' in front of an audience of directors.

- If appropriate, and if it is your style, descriptive and potent language is a powerful tool. Words create images and stir imaginations – words can paint a thousand pictures.

- Avoid jargon.

- Don't confuse or overload your content with information. Cut, cut and cut anything that does not add to your presentation – cut as if you were blasting rock with dynamite.

- Build a rhythm to your speech.

- Be creative and a bit different. Think outside the box.

- If appropriate, draw on personal experiences in your speech material.

- Find and choose the way of writing that works best for you – either write your presentation word for word, or just put together bullet points. The advantage of writing in full is that with the word count, you can more accurately determine the length and time of your speech.

- When you have delivered many presentations, and have written many different speeches, you can start developing and using a library of 'building blocks'. These are distinct sections of speeches, divided into subjects or themes, that can then be put together at very short notice to enable you to create a new, different and fresh-sounding speech.

Structuring And Organising Your Speech

- Most people will only remember 3 to 5 main points. Therefore, keep it simple – keep any really detailed information for handouts or a book or CD. Your main aim is to hook people into your subject matter, and keep them interested and engaged.

- There are many types of speech structures and outlines used by practised speakers, but all have a beginning, middle and end.

- What you are looking for is a striking and memorable opening, an interesting and stimulating middle, and a clear and strong conclusion.

- Try to grab your audience at the beginning. You could perhaps add suspense, or ask questions, tell a story, or say something startling about your subject.

- With your opening, don't be clichéd, predictable, apologetic, boring or cringeworthy.

- Keep your middle upbeat and appealing. Spend a similar amount of time on each main point within this section.

- Lead your audience through your material in a logical fashion – don't jump and jerk all over the place so that your speech is difficult to follow.

- Remember the classic old adage – make a point and then tell a story (and vice versa). People will always remember a well-told story, and if you hang your important points or message on a story, the chances are people will not only remember the story itself, but also the point you were making with it. (A bit more on stories in a minute.)

- Your conclusion or summary is the last thing people will hear, so make it memorable. Don't let your speech fizzle out like a damp squib.

- If you are using notes for your presentation, at least try to memorise your introduction and conclusion. You will then come across as someone who knows their subject, and it will also give you more confidence in your delivery.

Using Stories

■ Storytelling is the most powerful weapon in your public speaking armoury. It enables you to make that fantastic connection with an audience – empathy.

■ Storytelling is an essential aspect of speech-making. Whether you want to win new business, persuade an audience with your points of view or simply leave a lasting message, using stories is one of the most effective ways to influence people.

■ Storytelling reaches the places that PowerPoint presentations, facts and figures, reams of data and random motivational quotes plucked from the ether of random motivational quotes can never hope to reach.

■ If you want to captivate your audience and really get your message across with power and impact when delivering your speech, presentation or pitch, then you really need to think about telling a story.

■ It is even better if you can draw on personal experiences for your stories. People like personalised stories – they do not want to see some emotionless and detached corporate robot. These will also help differentiate you and make you stand out.

Using Humour

- Appropriate humour is a fantastic tool when used in the right places, for people often learn most when they are having a laugh and some fun. Humour also helps you win an audience over and puts people at ease.

- Humour must only be used if appropriate, though – for instance, you wouldn't want to use it while making a redundancy announcement.

- Do not try to be a comedian if humour doesn't come naturally (especially with lame jokes). Do not tell inappropriate jokes that may offend or embarrass, or put in a gag for a gag's sake.

- That said, everyone has the ability to be funny – humour is everywhere. Anyone can do gentle humour that will make an audience warm to them.

- Exaggeration of real events and characters is an easy way to make people laugh and smile. Timing of delivery and facial expressions are also key.

Your Speech Or Presentation

How To Say It

Delivery / Manner

- Find which way works best for you when learning your speech – for instance, memorising just the key facts from bullet points or learning rote-style most of the content. Whatever process you choose, it will become easier and more familiar the more you speak and present.

- Be positive before and when you get up there – if you are feeling or looking downbeat or lacking confidence, this will show. Don't look like you're going to the guillotine.

- The most important thing is to look like you want to be up there.

- Be in charge of and command the speaking area – that's your domain. For the time you are up there, you own it!

- Whatever the purpose or subject of your speech, the aim is the same – to create empathy and rapport with the audience.

- Come across as a normal and nice person.

- Make sure your tone, message and delivery style suit the occasion and your audience.

- If the occasion calls for it (as most do), have some spark and energy. Be enthusiastic and upbeat – no one wants to see or hear a dullard.

- Be sincere. Say what you mean and believe.

- Try to let your audience feel your speech, not just hear it.

- Be original.

- Be memorable – for all the right reasons.

- Don't be afraid to show your emotions. People do not want to see some corporate automaton.

- Make sure you're not boring. Don't waffle.

- Remember, it's okay to be nervous and it's okay to make mistakes. Put things into context – what's the worst that can happen? After all, it's only a speech; you're not jumping out of a plane without a parachute, or facing a firing squad!!!

- Don't be apologetic or timid, or draw the audience's attention to any nerves or tension you may be feeling or to things that may not be going too well. Nerves are catching, and people remember mistakes if you tell them about them!

- Always remember that no normal audience thinks when you get up there, 'I hope this person is rubbish.' (Although actually, there is a place in Wisbech… but that's another story.)

- Remember your training and everything you have learnt, and you will be fantastic.

Appearance

■ Try to look the part – audiences naturally warm to someone who has put some thought and care into what they look like. Attract not distract attention.

■ Wear what you think is most appropriate for you and the occasion, and what you feel most comfortable, smart and confident in. Let your appearance make you feel good about yourself.

■ Match your appearance to the occasion – for instance, you wouldn't wear a suit and tie for a presentation at a punk rock convention. Similarly, you wouldn't wear a mini-skirt for a major business conference presentation (particularly if you're a man).

■ Do not wear anything that is overtly distracting. Watch open shirts, bright and too prominent jewellery, gaudy ties, very short skirts, medallions, scuffed or dirty shoes, skyscraper high heels, undone shoe laces, undone flies, ill-fitting suits, coloured shirts that will show sweat if there are very strong stage lights, etc.

Posture

- Let your pose be natural and relaxed, and what you feel most at ease with.

- Good posture will help you breathe and deliver more powerfully.

- Bad posture, slumping, slouching, hunching and tired and tensed muscles will often lead to poor voice projection as well as making you look uninspiring, and giving a poor impression to the audience.

- Also be aware of looking tired, hesitant, unsure, uncomfortable, or like a cardboard cut-out.

- Don't stand like you've been condemned, or look like a rabbit in the headlights.

- Watch the 'classic' distracting poses – 'the coin jangler' (hands in pockets jangling coins or keys), 'the policeman' (hands behind back – 'Evening all'), 'the soldier' (hands at side as if standing to attention), 'the fig leaf' (hands over you know where), 'the earring fiddler', 'the nose scratcher', 'the ear picker', 'the pen chewer', etc. Be aware of swaying to the side or rocking backwards and forwards on your heels.

- Work on developing your posture. Use relaxation techniques and exercises for stretching your muscles, loosening up and aligning the spine and head. Also, try to keep fit, as this will help.

- Look in a mirror when practising your posture. Get feedback from others.

Vocal Variety And Voice Projection

- Vocal variety colours and massively enhances your delivery, and helps keep your audience engaged and interested (and awake!).

- You want your voice to attract and draw people in like a fine and rich ruby wine – you don't want to be harsh, irritating and grating.

- You need to be articulate, pleasing to the ear, clear and audible, dynamic, natural sounding, impactful and well paced.

- Don't speak so fast that people can't follow what you are saying, or so slowly and monotone that you send people to sleep or make them want to slit their wrists. Similarly, don't speak so quietly that people can't hear you, or shout like a fishwife or boom like a foghorn.

- Watch 'erring' and 'umming' – do this too often and you will drive people to distraction and annoyance.

- Don't slur or mumble. Don't chew gum!

- Carry out some self-analysis to examine how your voice sounds when delivering a speech – get feedback from others.

- Learn how to pace your speeches for different audiences – this will enable you to adapt your vocal style for the types of audience you are speaking to.

- Ensure that all members of the audience can hear you clearly. Aim to 'hit the back wall'. Don't just talk 'in the throat' – use your stomach muscles, diaphragm, breath and voice muscles to push your voice up and out of you, and to project.

- Identify and become familiar with all the muscles and parts of the body that are used to support your voice. As well as the mouth and throat, these include the lower back flank muscles, the lower abdomen, intercostals, solar plexus, diaphragm and the resonators in your head.

- Effective voice projection will enable you to deliver relaxed and maximum output with the minimum effort. Developing voice projection is a continuous process which calls for a holistic-type approach, particularly with regards to breathing, relaxation and posture. Correct vocal and voice projection technique will come through repetition and practice.

- Do not forget the power of the pause. Pausing is a brilliant technique which enables the audience to fully take in important or thought-provoking points that you have made. Don't be afraid to pause for longer than you may feel comfortable with.

- Use vocal, breathing and relaxation exercises before giving your presentation – warm up your throat, jaw and lips. Relax your voice muscles and your whole body. Limber up, experiment, and find what exercises suit you best and when to do them.

- If you are using certain techniques and exercises, ensure you are doing them correctly, and that you aren't just including and practising bad habits. Think about seeking the advice of a voice coach or a fellow speaker who can help.

- Remember though, we are all different – we are not robots, so what suits one person may not necessarily suit someone else when developing techniques to improve voice projection and variety.

Eye Contact

- Your aim is to make everyone in your audience feel included, whether it's 3,000 people or 3. Everyone wants to feel that you are connecting with them – they do not want to feel left out. Even with a large audience it is possible to make everyone feel as if you are speaking directly to them.

- Eye contact also makes your audience more familiar for you – it removes 'the barrier of the unknown'.

- Eye contact is great for 'as you are speaking' feedback. You can get a sense of how your speech is going down – if it is going well, and you are holding the audience's attention, or if things aren't perhaps working as planned, thus giving you the opportunity to make some instant adjustments to what you are saying and to how you are saying it.

- Don't jump to conclusions, though, and misread eye contact from people. Learn by experience. Some audience members do sometimes give out unusual signals – for instance, they may look bored but are actually riveted, or they may look engrossed but are actually asleep with their eyes open.

- Do not just focus on one or a couple of people, and do not spend too long on one person – this will make them feel very uncomfortable, and also make others in the audience feel excluded and think, 'Hey, what's going on here, why aren't I being included?'

- Take in as many people as you can in the audience by randomly spending an appropriate amount of time on their area. Don't follow a predetermined or set pattern, but be as natural as possible and vary the areas of the room you are working. By the end of your presentation, aim to have covered the entire room, and the longer your speech, the more times you will have been able to do this.

- By all means, look for friendly faces, but do not spend too much time focusing on favourites, particularly when speaking in a work setting.

- Watch such things as 'the tennis match' (head moving quickly and repeatedly from right to left), looking above the audience, looking at some imaginary and unseen or random object in the distance, or looking down at the floor.

- If you know your material, and aren't using notes, the more time you can spend on eye contact.

- Have a friendly twinkle in your eyes.

- Do not have bloodshot, lifeless or wild eyes.

Body Language

- Have your face, body, actions and gestures reflect what your feelings are and what you are saying. Use of body language will add colour, depth and variety to your speech, and you will have more chance of coming across as sincere and enthusiastic.

- Aim for the audience to be receiving the same message through their eyes as through their ears. People will latch onto what they are seeing as well as hearing and will equate the two.

- Try to be natural and spontaneous. Work on eliminating any potentially distracting mannerisms.

Facial Expressions

■ You can give away what you are thinking or feeling by your expressions, and an audience will believe what they see.

■ Your genuineness, enthusiasm, friendliness, confidence and interest will show in your face, as will such negative feelings as nervousness, confusion, boredom and annoyance.

■ Always make your expressions appropriate to your speech content – you have to have the right facial expressions to match what you are saying. For instance, you wouldn't say, 'My dog died today,' whilst grinning like an idiot.

■ Don't look like you're going to your own execution. Watch licking or biting your lips, having a rictus grin, frowning or scowling inappropriately, etc.

■ If the occasion is appropriate (and most are), whatever your style, wear a smile! This will make you appear friendly and approachable.

Gestures

- Hand and arm gestures will add colour, depth and individuality to your presentation. They help support, illustrate, demonstrate and enhance what you are saying. They help you draw the audience in, and paint pictures about what you are saying.

- You can use gestures to demonstrate direction, location, size, weight, shape, comparison and importance.

- You need to have your gestures complement what you are saying, thinking or feeling. Keep them convincing, but also natural, spontaneous, well timed and relevant.

- Even if you need to develop your gestures, let them reflect your own personality and, above all, be comfortable with them. What's right for someone else may not work for you.

- Gestures don't need to be extravagant – subtle works as well.

- Make sure your gestures do not detract from what you are saying. Don't let them be false, unconvincing, vague or over-rehearsed. Watch off-putting and distracting habits such as fiddling with your ear or nose or a prop, adjusting your hair or clothing, etc.

Whole Body Movements

■ Watching a stationary and static speaker is like watching a monolith – it can be dull. However, constantly leaping around the stage like a jack-in-the-box can be as equally off-putting.

■ Try to put your whole body into your speech, and have your movements be natural, easy and smooth, yet purposeful. Your movements need to go together with and enhance what you are saying, not detract attention.

■ You can use your body movements to demonstrate or act out points within your speech.

■ Don't be artificial, ludicrously exaggerated or 'a slave to convention' (i.e. always religiously following the 'rule' of moving forwards to emphasise something and then stepping backwards when you have finished a point).

■ Don't intimidate and encroach on a person's personal space.

■ Watch too much pacing of the stage.

■ A nice tip is to use the stage by adopting a 'diamond shape' type movement, which you step in and out of naturally, smoothly, spontaneously and in different sequence.

Using Notes

- Try to avoid using notes if possible.

- If you do have to use notes, use prompt sheets with 16-point print or cards. Refer to them only when you need them.

- Don't have sheaves of notes like some weighty historical tome – if you have to, make sure they are connected together so that you don't get them muddled up.

- Don't read verbatim – remember, you are speaking, not reading. (I once saw someone even read out, 'Good morning, my name is (then their own name)' from notes!)

Watch Your Equipment – Props And Visual Aids, And Using Technology

■ If used properly, props and visual aids can be valuable tools. However, any visual aids must add to the presentation, not detract attention from it.

■ Choose carefully what sort of visual aids you want to use (i.e. PowerPoint, flipcharts, whiteboards, etc.) – this choice will depend upon the type of presentation, your delivery style, and the size and type of audience.

■ Whatever visual aids you choose, make sure they are clearly visible, and keep them simple and easy to look at.

■ Remember, with PowerPoint, the audience will often be drawn like moths to a flame to what is on a slide rather than to what you are saying, so do not overload slides with text or have too many slides – and under no circumstances just regurgitate lengthy text from a slide. If you do this, you may as well say, 'Here's my presentation – I'll sit down while you read it,' or just hand them a memory stick. (With PowerPoint, pictures with minimal text often work well.)

■ If you are using PowerPoint, don't stand in front of the screen so that people are reading the presentation on your shirt.

■ Also, if using 'technology', make sure it works. Test equipment thoroughly, and make sure you can still make your presentation if anything doesn't work. Have a backup plan for if things go wrong.

■ With microphones, test and try these out before your speech to ensure that everything is working properly, and watch for feedback / booming / breathiness. If using a contact mic, test beforehand that you can move around the stage without causing rustling, interference or having the sound cut out.

■ If you have sound and lighting people handling the technology, trust in these technicians.

Handling Q&A Sessions

- Question and Answer sessions are a great way of getting the audience participating.

- Leave enough time for the session. Let the audience know at the beginning of your speech that there will be time for questions at the end.

- Control the session – you are in charge. Do not let it 'run away from you' and turn into a free for all. Do not be rude or abrupt, though, nor 'cut anyone down'.

- Always be polite and respect your audience.

- It's a good technique to work on a 'hands up, please' basis when asking for questions.

- Listen carefully to the questions being asked – be genuinely interested in the question.

- Thank the questioner for the question, and when you have answered, say something like, 'I hope that has answered your question.' It's always nice as well to ask the questioner's name after initially addressing them as Sir or Madam.

- If a questioner speaks quietly, repeat the question so that everyone in the room knows what it is you are answering.

- Be honest – don't try to answer something if you don't know the answer. Say to the questioner you'll look into it, and if they give you their contact details you'll then get in touch with them with the answer.

- Don't put anyone down, or embarrass or offend anyone.

- Don't rise to any challenges or get into an argument over what may seem like an aggressive or confrontational question (these are very, very rare).

- When there's only time for one more question, say so.

Your Speech Or Presentation

Preparation

Know Your Material

- Remember the old adage– fail to prepare, prepare to fail.

- Know your material – if you speak about what you know, you're already on track and halfway there.

- Research and rehearse so that you know your subject inside out and can practically deliver it in your sleep. You need to practise until your presentation almost becomes a part of you, and seems to flow from your very being. You also need to balance this, though, with a degree of unrehearsed 'edge' and freshness.

- Rehearsing is a great form of editing and finding out what works.

- Get into the habit of rehearsing in front of a mirror, into a voice recorder, rehearsing really fast, and of practising silently, in your head.

- Rehearse in front of family, friends or colleagues, and ask for feedback.

- Focus on adding improvements step by step.

- Constant practice will help you eliminate any timing issues – i.e. overrunning or coming up too short.

- Learn to develop the skill to be able to adapt to circumstances that any timing challenges may present (e.g. at the last minute the organiser may say you only have 10 minutes in which to speak, not 20). Throw in some 'curveballs' when rehearsing to see how this works.

- If you are going to use notes or visual aids or technology, make sure you are comfortable and confident with them, and check that all your equipment works.

- On the day of the presentation, make sure you have rested and eaten properly.

- For your mental preparation, get plenty of daily relaxation and breathing exercises, plenty of positive visualisation, and building up of excitement and eagerness for the presentation.

Know The Venue

- Find out as much as possible in advance about the venue and agenda. How long will it take you to get there? What time will you be speaking?

- What will the room layout be like? Will you be using a microphone? Will there be a lectern / a stage / stage lights?

- Will there be anyone speaking before or after you? If so, who, and on what subjects?

- Remember your research on the audience you carried out when you first started writing your speech.

Getting Ready Before You Arrive

- In the preceding few days or even weeks before an important performance, be aware of the benefits of such things as exercise, stretching, sleep, rest, relaxation, and healthy and sensible eating and drinking.

- Get into the habit of getting yourself in the best possible frame of mind and physical well-being before your presentation.

- Use relaxation and confidence-boosting exercises, and resourcing and anchoring techniques. Use positive thinking and visualisation of yourself standing in the speaking area, giving a fantastic performance and receiving rapturous applause from a totally appreciative audience.

- Make sure you've got everything you need for your presentation. And don't forget those small personal backup things, such as bottled water, spare contact lenses, a toothbrush, paracetamol, etc.

At The Venue

- Arrive early.

- If you have the time, it's always nice to have a stroll and grab some fresh air before entering the venue.

- Get to know and become familiar with the room.

- Walk round, test any microphones, try out the visual aids, etc.

- If you haven't had chance to visit the venue before, make yourself aware of such things as: How are the acoustics? Is there any noise from the air conditioning? Will it be hot from heating or from stage lights while you are speaking? Will people be able to hear you at the back (test this out on someone before the room fills up)? Are there any squeaky floorboards in the speaking area? Will anyone in the audience have a restricted view so that you will have to adapt your stage positioning?

- When delivering your speech, be aware of time by being able to see a clock or watch.

- Make sure you have water near at hand when speaking.

- If you haven't already done so, check with the organiser if and how you are going to be introduced.

- Regarding alcohol before you speak (if you are speaking at, say, an after-dinner event, it is possible that there will be some drink flowing), it's highly recommended not to drink beforehand, although you need to know and be comfortable with your own threshold. (Rock bands before and during a gig are an exception, but would you expect a surgeon to have a few drinks before a major operation?)

- Know the audience and greet some members as they arrive. It is easier to talk to friendly faces with whom you are at least a little familiar than to total strangers. Don't come across as 'The Speaker'.

- If after dinner speaking, watch overeating before you speak.

- Avoid sports or energy drinks – too much sugar will combine with any adrenaline surges.

- If it works for you, it's a good idea to eat an apple or banana 20 or 30 minutes before you go on – this helps with energy and blood sugar levels.

- Go to the bathroom 10 or 15 minutes before you speak. Also, check your teeth (that's why to bring a toothbrush), your nose, your flies, etc.

- Don't forget your voice exercises and warm-ups, and stretching / limbering-up of neck and shoulders.

- Remind yourself that you are there to give the audience the gift of your experience and knowledge. Develop your own psyching-up and anchoring routines.

- Get in the mindset to 'own the stage' and to create your own 'zone of invincibility' once you're up there.

- If for any reason you haven't had the chance to check everyone can hear, ask the audience right at the beginning, and then make any necessary adjustments and changes to your volume.

- Remember again, do not overrun – think of the audience and any other speakers.

- **Remember all your training and preparation, and you will be brilliant.**

Thanks and acknowledgements

Sharon, for all the fantastic and wonderful
support which I could not do without.
Lydia and Gabrielle.
Mum and Dad.
Jill and Ray.
All my friends and fellow speakers at
Toastmasters International.